Hereos
~~Heroes~~ Journey

RSO (oil)
purified THC
edibles

{Psychology:}
The Stuff You Can Really Use

BRADLEY W. RASCH

iUniverse, Inc.
Bloomington

Psychology: The Stuff You Can Really Use

iUniverse books may be ordered through booksellers or by contacting:

iUniverse
1663 Liberty Drive
Bloomington, IN 47403
www.iuniverse.com
1-800-Authors (1-800-288-4677)

ISBN: 978-1-4759-0084-2 (sc)
ISBN: 978-1-4759-0086-6 (e)

Library of Congress Control Number: 2012904950

Printed in the United States of America

iUniverse rev. date: 3/27/2012

To the reader,
most especially students of psychology.
You know who you are.

Introduction

Having worked as a psychologist for over thirty years and having had the opportunity to teach the subject at the college level for a like amount of time, I have discovered what this field has to offer that is really useful and interesting. From this book, you can gain information you can actually use to enhance your life, understand yourself and others better, and be a real asset to any group engaged in a deep discussion of psychology. Let's get started.

Social x

Freud Was Right
(About Some Things At Least)

Sigmund was, in some ways, an odd man. He was obsessed with sex and discussed things like penis envy. He used cocaine quite a bit. His beard did not flatter him. He did stumble upon something important, however, and made a valuable contribution as a result.

Freud talked about the importance of love and work to achieving fulfillment and happiness. Indeed, in our culture, this is true for most of us (unless we are a member of the idle rich without a sense of noblesse oblige or work for the Department of Motor Vehicles). The vast majority of us seek to love and work as well as we can. We want to love and support others, and we want to contribute and excel at our work, no matter what it may be. To a great degree, we are hardwired to judge ourselves, and we derive a great degree of satisfaction if we do these things well or at least to the best of our ability given life's circumstances.

In our culture, one of the first things you ask someone is, "What do you do?" We derive so much of our identity from our occupation—so much so that retired people may be uncomfortable with this question, as the answer may be "Nothing." Half of their identity may be gone. For some, especially high achievers, retirement can be difficult. They may feel insignificant. As people grow older, there is a greater sense of urgency to have made your mark by contributing to your field of endeavor and being there for your loved ones in their times of need.

When someone is unhappy, there is a good chance that he feels unfulfilled in one of these key areas. Cut him some slack, and help him excel in those areas. That's a good way to love.

Christopher Cross Was Right Too

mindful meditation

Christopher Cross once wrote a song called "Sailing." It wasn't really about boating, however. His point is that we all need hobbies. They allow us to relax, escape, reduce stress, and go to another place. Indeed, as he says in his song, "The canvas can do miracles." He was on to something there. Whether it is painting, sailing, collecting coins, or sewing, hobbies do provide a sense of fulfillment. They allow us to relax, reduce stress, and improve our mental health (unless you're a Cubs fan). They also allow us to find and relate to others with a similar passion. In many cases, a hobby provides a common link between generations. My father took me to see a young rookie named Pete Rose play for the Cincinnati Reds. I took my daughter to see Pete in his last year in the major leagues. Boy, did he have a long career. My love of baseball contributed to many passionate discussions with both my father and my daughter, both big baseball fans. Christopher, thanks for your contribution.

hobbies:
run marathons

I took Ryan to see Cal Ripkin before he retired.

Happy sports memories w/ boys.

Took Erik to see Hersey Hawkins #33 while Sonics still in Seattle

AND Michael Jordan's last game in Seattle

+ M's @ Kingdome.

Mom - Garth Brooks @ WSU (road trip) + Bonamy's Heart @ Puyallup Fair

Sorry, Paula, You Were Wrong

Paula Abdul, you are a great singer, and you have made tremendous videos and some great contributions to pop culture. Though I enjoyed your songs about opposites being attracted to one another, in many cases that is not true. Most people, on some level, are attracted to people similar to themselves in terms of values, interests, background, and even in level of attractiveness. Having things in common helps build a relationship. I'm not saying that we should not involve ourselves with or befriend people who are dissimilar to us. We just need to work harder to have the attraction work and to find common interests. We are also attracted to people we have frequent contact with, people who are physically attractive, and folks we know like us. (We tend to think they are good judges of character.)

Can't We All Just Get Along?[1]

Apparently not, Rodney. Most people are let go from jobs because they have trouble getting along with people in the workplace, not because of technical incompetence. Those who can answer Rodney's question in the affirmative will have more stable employment, a higher ceiling, and a lot less stress in their life.

Jamie Farr, the actor who played Klinger in *M*A*S*H*, wrote an excellent autobiography. An accomplished actor, the host of a great golf tournament, and arguably the world's most beloved cross-dresser, he made an important point in this book. He stated that it is important to wake up each day and realize that a good percentage of people take an a**hole pill every morning when they get up. One of the great accomplishments in life is realizing that they do this, you can't do anything about it, and the sooner you realize that the better.

---

1 Rodney King

4

Self-Defeating Urination

Perl's once said, "If you have one foot in the past and one foot in the future, you're pissing on the present." Judge Judy is often fond of saying, "Don't pee on my leg and tell me it's raining." My urologist says I have an enlarged prostate.

Let's deal with Perls's urination proclamation. Indeed, if we focus too much on the past, something we cannot change, and worry excessively about the future, we are missing most of the present. And we are certainly not enjoying it. Living, as they say, "in the moment" is something we should all strive to do. Consciously deciding to do this every day and working on it is a great way to live a happier life.

This is not to say we should not plan long term or prepare for important things. We should also enjoy reminiscing about good things, but we should not focus on the past or future to the detriment of now.

Next week, I have this prostrate exam, and ...

Your Pants and the Damn Dog

Dr. Sydney Freidman, the psychiatrist who saw through the aforementioned Corporal Klinger, once gave this advice to the stressed-out medical personnel of the 4077th. "Ladies and gentleman, take my advice, pull down your pants, and slide on the ice." This was great advice by a good, but fictional, psychiatrist. All too often, we do not do simple things that we regret not doing the rest of our lives. If those things won't hurt anyone, do as Nike suggests—Just do it.

When I retired as a school psychologist after thirty-four long years, on my last day, I decided I should go down to the office and page myself. I also decided I should bolt a plaque above a room naming the room after me. I am glad I did these things. Had I not, I would have regretted it the rest of my life and would have missed an opportunity to feed into stereotypes about psychologists. Now generations of people will ask, "Who was that nut?"

When visiting the Hoover Dam, I had an opportunity to buy a footlong dam dog that came with a Hoover Dam hard hat. I did not, and I have regretted it ever since.

Pull down your pants, and bite the dog.

Gomer Pyle, Vampires, and the Flying Nun

Does it concern you that everyone seems obsessed with vampires? That television and the silver screen seem to be all about vampires 24/7? Does the national interest in reality TV suggest a dumbing down of our populace, especially when we are faced, quite possibly, with events every bit as serious as the Great Depression and the Cold War?

Before you become overly worried about our seemingly wrong-headed obsession with trash TV during these trying times, let me remind you of something. During the height of the Vietnam War, when civil unrest associated with that conflict was ripping apart the very fabric of our society, the *Gomer Pyle* TV show was extremely popular. It never once mentioned the Vietnam War. Was that a reflection of our collective stupidity? No, it was an escape. Just as the vampire craze is now. It was no more an indicator of a low collective IQ than our obsession with vampires is today. As a society, we need an escape, a little mental relaxation from the current stressful climate.

I do not know how to explain the flying nun.

Bob Dylan and David Bowie

Bob Dylan said, "The times they are a-changin." David Bowie sang, "Ch-ch-ch changes." We are only hardwired to stress about change if we choose to be. Certainly, from what we do for a living, to the events around us and technology, times are changing at light speed all around us, faster than they have ever before. The greatest skill, passion, or characteristic each of us can have in this time is embracing the fact that the world is changing quickly and choosing to enjoy it.

We need to accept that change happens, make it a priority to anticipate and adapt to inevitable change, and learn to love it. Perceive it as an adventure. There's no need to skydive or seek thrills in these times. If we view change as a hobby, a passion, we will enjoy our journey so much more.

Robert Burns once said, "The best laid schemes o' mice and men often go astray." This is truer than ever. If we accept this as the new normal and choose to embrace it, we are far better off. Yes, we should plan, but we should also enjoy the challenge of being flexible and look forward to having to reinvent ourselves periodically.

It's Always Something.
If It Ain't One Thing, It's Another.[2]

Misery loves company, but nobody loves a miserable person. When we are anxious or stressed out, research shows that we want to be with other people. If we are a veteran, we like to talk with other veterans about our mutual experiences. If we receive a cancer diagnosis, we look to spend time with others similarly afflicted. We lessen stress when we are with someone, preferably a person who has been through or is going through what we are dealing with.

That being said, a chronic complainer, someone who always seems to be a victim or perpetually has something to complain about, can dampen the mood of others. People do not want to be brought down and generally do not like to be around the chronically unhappy.

---

2   Roseanne Roseannadanna

Memories Light the Corners of My Mind[3]

Do you ever notice you infrequently remember someone's name after you have been introduced? Bad memory? In part. But you can fix it.

When we are introduced to someone, we are not really focusing on what is being said. We are busy planning our witty remark. That lack of focus, not really attending, is why we do not remember his name. If we make a conscious effort to focus when introduced, hear someone's name, and repeat it a few times in our "mind's ear," we will remember it. Both politicians and salespeople know this.

Dale Carnegie once said, "There is no sweeter word in the English language than one's own name." He was right. If we are in a circle of people and each person takes a turn introducing himself and shares a little bit about himself, we will remember less about the person who spoke just before us than we will about what anyone else said. Again, it is because we are focusing on what we are going to say, not on what they are saying. Knowing this and adjusting for it can improve our memory.

Now, if I could only find my car keys.

---

3   Barbara Streisand

One Man's Fault Is Another Man's Lesson

Whenever we see someone do or say something, we always ask ourselves, "Why did he do or say that?" We must, whether we are aware of it or not, attribute his actions to some cause. Sometimes we decide someone did something because he is that way on the inside. At other times, we decide that somebody acted in the manner he did because the situation forced him to.

If you do something nice for someone, you hope he attributes your behavior to you being nice on the inside. If you do something rather mean, you would probably hope that he sees the situation you were in or the fact you were carrying out a superior's wishes as influencing your behavior.

When people make a judgment as to why you behaved as you did, more often than not, they will determine that you did or said something because of who you are on the inside. Not because the situation might have forced you to do it. Most of us make this mistake frequently. Keep this in mind when you have to do or say something that someone might perceive as negative. Remember, people usually make this common mistake of attribution. When trying to understand the actions of others, remember you will frequently make this error of judgment as well.

Additionally, we tend to assume that people do things for the same reasons we do. This also tends to make us err in our assessment of others.

When a Man Gives His Opinion, He's a Man. When a Woman Gives Her Opinion, She's a Bitch[4]

We like things simple. We do not like to think too much. That characteristic is hardwired into our DNA. This desire to keep it simple explains why stereotypes are so prevalent. It is easier to maintain a stereotype, even if it is inaccurate, than to judge people individually.

We do tend to evaluate people of an entire group based on our experiences with (or even what we have heard about) just one person from that group. The resulting stereotypes are remarkably resistant to change. Even after a lifetime of experience, that should dispel them.

When a large group of people has an inaccurate stereotype about a group, they can actually make that stereotype come true. When I was in high school, many held the stereotype that football players were dumb, arrogant, rude jocks, based on the behavior of one young man on the team. As a result, the student body treated the football players rather rudely and in a condescending manner. The treatment the football players received from the student body changed the behavior of the people on the team. They had no choice but to stick to themselves and avoid nonathletes. Such is the insidious power of stereotypes.

By the way, students engaged in extracurricular activities obtain better grades and have higher graduation rates.

---

4   Bette Davis

Most People Shoot the Mule

When I was a young high school student, the plan toward most books that were required reading was the following:

1. See the movie.
2. If there were no movie, buy the Cliffs Notes.
3. If Cliffs had no notes, read the book.

Fortunately, one of the books we were required to read was not made into a movie, and Cliffs did not get around to writing notes about it. In this post-Civil War book, a white Southern family worked a subsistence farm next to the family of a newly freed slave. The former slave's farm was much more successful, and he and his family were more prosperous. They could even afford a mule, which the white family could not.

The white man suffered mentally from this disparity and felt like a failure. The black family's mule ownership particularly hurt him. The community had a great deal of disrespect for this white farmer, but not nearly as much disrespect as he had for himself. After seasons of anguish, he finally dealt with the problem and felt better as a result. He shot the black family's mule.

This story resonated with me. As I trained to be a psychologist, I learned that most people gauge their happiness and develop their self-esteem by comparing themselves to others. Many people feel better if someone is below them. A few of us have evolved as people to the point where we gauge our self-worth and happiness in relation to where we are vis-à-vis our own potential.

Sadly, most of us shoot the mule.

Confession Is Good for the Soul

Generally, we feel a lot better when we unburden ourselves and try to set things right. Allow me the opportunity to do so. The bottom line here is this: I would not be here today, literally, if not saved from one of my mistakes. It happened just when my career was beginning.

When I started out as a school psychologist back in the early 1970s, I worked in a very rural area. Indeed, the town I lived in was so small that even the yogurt did not have culture. Coming from Chicago, it was surprising to me that the town had but one stoplight. I started here because this largely rural state had a well-deserved impeccable reputation for valuing and supporting education. It was then—and is now—a state of great innovation in the field of education.

My position started in late August, but it was suggested that I (along with all the other new employees) volunteer to be counselors for a two-week summer camp for mentally handicapped children at a beautiful lake resort in the northern part of the state. My new boss ran this camp, so it seemed prudent to volunteer. (Actually, I would have done so anyway, even if it had not been mandatorily voluntary.)

My presence at this camp was especially important because the preponderance of handicapped children tend to be male, and most school employees tend to be female. A male counselor was definitely needed. My cabin had twelve mentally handicapped young men of high school age. All were well behaved, fun loving, and in need of a great deal of attention and assistance. One of them, John, was an exceptional athlete. This kid did every sport well. You name the sport, and he excelled at it. I did not know of his great athletic talent until after the first day in camp. To be precise, I learned of his gift the first evening.

14

After our first busy day of camp, all the kids and staff went down to the lakeshore just before sunset. We sat around a bonfire, sang camp songs, and watched the sun beginning to set across the lake. As we were singing, a speedboat skimmed the surface at a great rate of speed about a half-mile out on the lake. John, one of my charges, stood up, pointed at the boat, and yelled "Motorboat!" He ran to the end of the pier, dived in, and started swimming after the boat. John was my responsibility. I screamed at him to return, but he would not. I had no choice but to run to the end of the pier myself and swim after John. John and I were very different, mostly in our swimming ability. He was a great swimmer. I, on my best days, am a mediocre swimmer in a pool. I had never before swum in a lake. (For full disclosure, in a pool, I am a mediocre swimmer only in the shallow end.)

I swam as urgently as I could to save this poor boy, not gaining on him but trying my level best. Periodically, I would shout out and plead with him to come back. I could hear the entire staff yelling for John to turn around and come back. He kept going. We were out farther and farther, and it was getting increasingly dark. Not being a good swimmer or in nearly as good condition as John was, despite the adrenalin rush of trying to reach John and save him, I realized I did not have the stamina to go any farther to catch John and I had nothing left to make it to shore either. The only thing I could do was yell out to John, "Help me, John. I can't make it back." The staff thought this was a brilliant ploy to get the good-natured John to turn back and help me. John, being the good young man and great athlete he was, dutifully turned around and towed me to shore. The staff, my new boss, and everyone else complimented me for using a little psychology to save John. The kudos were coming so quickly that I was unable to tell the real story. John's parents thanked me when they picked him up at the end of camp for allowing him to save me. This improved his self-esteem immensely. It is thirty-five years too late, but the truth of the matter is that John really did save me.

There. I feel better. Thanks.

Dumb and Dumber?

N o, not really. But this still needs to be said. I have included a reprint of an article I published many years ago. It is as true today as it was then. I respect and admire students. Please do not get me wrong. But there is a lesson to be learned here.

The Buttafuocoization of America

As a part-time instructor in the social studies departments of two community colleges, I enjoy keeping my students abreast of current news that relates to the areas that we are studying. I even like to call their attention to recent news article that are interesting but not exactly related to what we are covering in the course.

Two years ago, I read an article in a well-respected weekly news magazine that infuriated me. It angered me so much that I brought it to my classes to expose it as an example of poor research. I was going to band together with my students to prove this article a fraud.

The article stated that, given four choices, a large percentage of college students could not correctly identify which nation we fought during World War II. The correct choice among the four was Germany. It also stated that a very large percentage of students could not correctly identify an entire continent on an unmarked map.

I introduced this challenge to my students with a sense of righteous indignation. I suggested we go about proving the magazine wrong (albeit in a nonscientific way) and then write a letter with an attitude to the magazine's editor. The class agreed with gusto.

We decided to prove the magazine wrong on its first finding, that a large percentage of American students could not properly identify our enemy of World War II. I gave the class a multiple-choice question asking them to pick the nation we fought during World War II. The options were:

A. Mexico
B. Vietnam
C. Russia
D. Germany

The majority of the class felt that the United States had fought Russia during World War II. The magazine had been vindicated in its judgment of American students. I knew that it was incumbent on me to make a riveting and eloquent statement about what had just happened. I felt this statement to be so important that I paused a moment to sort things out. Before I could begin my sermon addressing this event, one of my students spoke up. The student had emigrated from Russia to the United States less than a year before taking this class. He said: "No wonder our nations have had such problems over the last forty-five years. Our two countries, Russia and America, fought side by side against the Germans. Our country used arms supplied by America to do it."

My planned sermon would have lacked the impact of this young man's statement. For the remainder of the semester, students came to class exceptionally well prepared.

Since this event, I have given each of my classes a similar quiz. Afterward, I tell them the story of my attempt to prove the magazine wrong. The last such quiz I administered (in the fall of 1993) asked the students to identify or define in a short-answer format the following people or things:

A. NAFTA
B. Al Gore
C. Mother Theresa
D. Joey Buttafuoco

Less than one-third of the class correctly identified Al Gore. (Vice presidents certainly manage to maintain a low profile.) One hundred percent of the class correctly identified Joey Buttafuoco. Not one student knew what NAFTA was.

After this quiz, I told the students why I had given it to them. I shared with them the story of the Russian immigrant and the effect that his words had on my class a few years ago. We discussed at length what had just occurred, and we came up with many reasons why the students were so familiar with Joey Buttafuoco and so unfamiliar with NAFTA. One thing I learned as a result of the class discussion was that all three major television networks had aired made-for-television movies about Joey Buttafuoco. I also learned that Joey was planning to do a book and a music video.

Say it ain't so, Joe. And we will all live happily ever NAFTA.

Consequences: A Forgotten Concept

Veterans of World War I marched on Washington in 1932 to demand a bonus that Congress had voted on in 1924. The Bonus Army apparently thought that an eight-year delay in their bonus was a bit long, even for the federal government. Some of the veterans constructed a shantytown on Anacostia Flats. This created a public eyesore and made a generally bad impression on visitors to the nation's capital. The Hoover administration branded the veterans as communists and criminals and sent for General Douglas MacArthur and seven hundred troops, who promptly burned the veterans out. In the process, exposure to tear gas killed an eleven-week-old baby.

Compare this to our seeming inability to come up with a solution to one of our most pressing contemporary problems, our crime-ridden streets, beset by gangs of teenagers armed with sophisticated weaponry battling openly for control of the drug trade. In spite of frantic pleas from urban mayors, no help is forthcoming, certainly nothing on the order of General MacArthur. Instead, the National Guard meets on weekends at local armories and prepares for God knows what. Invasion by the Canadians, I suppose. Stray bullets fired by the neighbor's kids kill modern babies, not tear gas.

It's quite a difference in governmental response to civil disobedience. You might say that. And you might also add that the Hoover response of 1932 was an overreaction, while our modern-day officials appear to prefer underreaction. Although we may condemn both extremes, we shouldn't be too harsh in our judgment, for the social atmosphere in which we find ourselves largely determines our reaction to external stimuli (in this case, gangs of people in the streets). The 1930s were years in which a worldwide depression created a fear of communism and bred a law-and-order mentality that is quite different from the way we view law enforcement today. The 1990s, by contrast, have been marked by a social void in which we seem incapable of ascribing guilt to anyone. Given the changes in social atmosphere, the responses of individuals in the two decades are largely predictable: call out the troops, or call out the social workers.

Does our contemporary social landscape influence relationships on a more personal level? We need only turn to television to find some clues. After all, television is a good yardstick by which to measure what our current society things is socially acceptable (unless you believe that the media leads the public rather than mirror its views). I happen to think we are shown, via television, just what the people who produce the broadcasts think we want to see. Certainly, that is what the sponsors are banking on. Producers select what they will and will not broadcast by studying us in great detail. They know what we will stomach and what we will reject. (That is why a series titled *Combat* was popular just prior to the heating-up of the Vietnam War but not after the war had escalated. Somehow, war stories lose their appeal when our sons and fathers are coming home in flag-draped coffins.)

Let's begin by looking back a few years, when some well-meaning, anticrime types ran a spot on television that I view as sort of an omen of things to come. In the spot, which appeared amid an array of other commercials, a character was featured who had left his keys in his car, only to have some passing youth steal it. At the conclusion of this spot, a voice intoned, "Take your car keys. Don't help a good boy go bad." More recently, a television commercial for a popular breakfast cereal featured a disgruntled teenager chiding her father with the words "You're pressuring us!"

Although several years separate them, these two commercials are a far cry from President Hoover's reaction to the Bonus Army. They show, in a very real way, the direction we are going with our children, a direction we can see clearly by examining the messages we send to our young people every day. Subtle and sure, these messages creep into the fabric of popular culture, into the media, into our jargon, and into our rationales for social relationships and interactions.

Let us look more carefully at the first commercial I referred to. Notice that the message seems to be that the guilt for the car theft lies more with the man who forgot his keys than with the boy who actually stole the vehicle. What a bumbling character that driver is! He not only left his keys in the ignition, but he foolishly transformed a good boy into a bad boy. Now, a thinking viewer might ask, "What is a good boy doing in this guy's car in the first place?" or "Wouldn't a good boy bring the keys to the police station rather than steal the vehicle?" Of course, we're not supposed to ask such questions. Instead, we're supposed to view the crime as some type of strange interactive enterprise in which the victim contributes as much as the criminal does. This leaves any distinction between the two characters essentially vague and meaningless. The producers of this spot have created an essentially cynical statement: "Virtue is lack of opportunity, and criminal victimizations are a logical penalty for forgetfulness."

In the second television spot I described, the child engages in a curious role reversal in which an adult, in this case, a parent, is chewed out for asking a few simple, inoffensive questions. In addition, pressure comes off rather like child abuse. Consequently, we are left to assume that it is wrong for adults to put pressure on children. If we draw this point out to its logical end, terms such as "suggestion," "advice," and a score of others must also be seen in a negative light when used with children. Apparently, we are to deal with our children on a subliminal level. Sure.

Can our modern hesitancy to place blame, when combined with our apparent inability to correct our children, lead to a situation in which the concept of consequences becomes foreign?

Let us turn our attention to a real-life story. At the center of this story is a boy, whom I will refer to as N. Not only did he have the misfortune of being burdened with a behavioral disorder during his early years, he grew up in our contemporary society in which dispensing reasonable consequences in response to negative actions is viewed as socially backward and unenlightened. N seldom encountered consequences of any kind until he was eighteen years of age. By that time, it was too late.

The school and the parents in this case provided no tangible consequences in response to N's negative behaviors. When N exhibited aggressive traits at age five, his parents adopted a defensive stance characterized by such expressions as, "Boys will be boys" and other shopworn phrases that equate bullying behaviors with male rites of passage. N was "too young to know better," and nobody wanted to put any pressure on him. Sound familiar?

Classified as behaviorally disordered while still in elementary school, N was never suspended for his antisocial acts because his behavior was related to his handicap and thus beyond the scope of punishment when viewed through the intricate prism of special education law. N's parents hired an attorney and an advocate to protect his rights.

These rights eventually came to include the following: never giving N a grade below a C, allowing him to use inappropriate and abusive language when speaking to his teachers, letting him break another student's nose with no tangible consequences, and allowing him to remain on a local youth baseball team even though he threw his bat at a pitcher and kicked an umpire. After leaving school, N was employed at his father's business, where his father openly fired other employees who had the nerve to complain about his son's abusive behaviors. Eventually, N was arrested for assault after he pushed people out of line at a convenience store so he could get to the front. He calmly told the arresting officers what he'd heard all his life. He was compulsive and couldn't help it. Somehow, these excuses failed to make an impression on the police officers, and they took him away in their squad car, much to N's amazement. Gee whiz, fellas.

Now, is N unique in the contemporary social landscape? I suggest that the answer is a resounding no. Not only does our society fail to put appropriate pressure on people to alter negative behaviors, it fails particularly during that most crucial time of a human being's life, the early years. We should feel sorry for N because our spineless philosophies cheated him. I do not mean to suggest here that we should not cut some slack for a child with a behavioral disorder, but I do believe that we should refrain from insulating him entirely from the idea that actions have consequences. Even our ultrapermissive society cannot insulate him forever, as N learned that day in the convenience store. If we fail to provide adequate consequences for children who suffer from behavioral disorders, not only will we fail to eliminate their dysfunctions, we will create socially stunted individuals who will be unable to function in an adult world.

I am saying that such supposedly antiquated ideas as the importance of responsibility, recognizing one's guilt, and accepting the consequences are not out of date after all. Nor is pressure of a constructive sort necessarily a bad thing. We need to be more demanding of our children, but in a gentle and loving way. We need to say more often, "Sorry, but you'll have to accept the consequences."

If we can't agree to do at least this much, then we will have to fight our way through every major American city and every small town and rural crossroads. Who know? We might even grow to love living in the new Tombstone, especially if we're avid fans of the Old West.

Just one final thing. If you're one of the timid breed who can find an excuse for just about anything and can't bear to say no to children, don't be surprised if our youngsters turn out like Billy the Kid.

David Letterman Is on to Something: Top Ten Lists Are Good

The following are ten philosophies to have and practice that will enhance your life:

1. **Volunteer.** People who give to and help others often benefit much more than those they are helping.

2. **Improve your confidence.** Know your abilities. Build on your strengths, and compensate for your weaknesses.

3. **Be at peace with yourself.** As the friends of Bill W. and Dr. Bob say, change what you can change and accept what you can't change.

4. **Eat right and exercise.** The computer programming maxim "garbage in, garbage out" applies to nutrition as well. We feel better when we eat better. Not only does regular exercise improve your physical health, it affects your mental health as well. Physical exercise is just as or more effective than talk therapy or drugs in improving many cases of mild depression.

5. **Develop a real budget and stick to it.** Financial problems are one of the most significant stressors we face and a special stressor in the context of marriage. Lessen stress by coming to an understanding of the difference between wants and needs.

6. **Do not forget family and friends.** Make time for them. You will regret it if you do not.

7. **Give/Accept help.** A friend in need is a friend indeed.

8. **Understand and manage your stress.** Know what stresses you, find ways to cope with stress, and use what techniques work for you.

9. **Know/Express your moods.** Know how you are feeling, and express those feelings in safe, constructive, and appropriate ways.

24

10. **Share your problems with others in the same situation.** When something very significant stresses you, find others going through the same thing to share experiences with. You will be glad you did, and so will they.

Shame on Us

Psychologists and social workers (our professional cousins) are guilty of something that has perplexed me for decades. When a parent commits a senseless and appalling act of parenting and the state removes the child from the home, this is often accomplished with the complicity of psychologists and social workers. This is not my pet peeve. What usually happens next is.

Mental health professionals frequently recommend that the mistreated child be placed with his grandparents. Really? Did the grandparents do such a good job raising their child, the parent who committed an act so bad that the state removed the child from his custody?

This is not an indictment of grandparents. I am one. It just seems odd that this is the common default recommendation. Should there not be some consideration at least of other possible options? We should not fall into the complacency of doing something or approving of something because it has always been done that way. Yet, we often do.

Depressed Veterinarian

Bob was a happy camper in high school. He was a star student and volunteered twenty hours a week at an animal hospital. He was well on his way to a worthy goal, becoming a veterinarian. Bob knew he had to get excellent grades to get into a good university. He was successful. He was accepted to a great college and received perfect grades. He aced the high-stakes test to get into vet school.[5] Bob was happy because he had a goal and he was making progress. Bob was accepted to veterinary school. He lived his dream. There was not a happier person on the planet when he was training to be a vet. How many of us set a tough goal and live it?

After vet school, Bob soon became severely depressed. People who knew and loved him were bewildered. He had achieved his lifelong dream. He was a vet, a dream that had dominated his entire life. How could this be?

When we have goals that are important to us and we are progressing toward them, we are happy. It gives us purpose and a great sense of accomplishment and satisfaction. It enhances our lives. But after he graduated, Bob had no goals, nothing to work for, no direction. The absence of goals and moving toward them depressed Bob. Bob set some new goals, and once again, he became a happy, driven man.

We need goals, and we need to be progressing toward them. In their absence, we are adrift.

---

5   In those days, it was a lot harder to get into a veterinary school compared to medical or dental school, along with the fact that there are far fewer veterinary schools than medical and dental schools. In fact, many physicians and dentists were frustrated vets who could not get into vet school.

But He Was Wrong About the Edsel

Henry Ford famously said, "Think you can; think you can't. Either way, you will be right." Ford was on to something here. Positive mental attitude, believing you can, self-confidence, or however you want to describe it is important to success. Studies show that one's confidence level can often exceed the importance of intelligence and sometimes even motivation in terms of achievement. His thoughts about the Edsel? Not so much.

While we are at it here, Thomas Edison was right on when he said genius is 90 percent perspiration and 10 percent inspiration. There is no substitute for putting in the time and doing the hard work. Research shows that people who can delay their need for immediate gratification achieve better grades, have higher earnings, and are happier people. They are the ones who studied Friday night as opposed to attending the Three Dog Night concert when they were in college.

Stages

We all go through various stages in life. At each stage, we wrestle with different demons, and we have unique priorities.

Very early in life, when we are in or just out of diapers, it is important for us to trust others in order to trust the world. It is important we find the world a nurturing place emotionally, physically, and spiritually. As toddlers, we strive to become independent, that is, autonomous.

When in school, we compare ourselves to others. We know that academic success is important. That is really drilled into us. I guarantee you that every first grader can tell you who is in the low, middle, or high reading group. Our perception of how we competed during these years can influence our level of confidence to some degree for a lifetime.

As adolescents, we need to develop a plan, at least in a general sense, of what we are going to do with our lives and a plan to obtain the skills to do so. It's no small undertaking. Further, we must believe that we will indeed become autonomous, self-supporting adults. As young adults, we desperately need a sense of intimacy with others, acceptance, and possibly intimacy with one special person.

In middle age, we have a strong need to give birth to something that will outlive us. This can be a child, but it is not just that. It could be contributing to our field, mentoring younger people, or having an opportunity to pass on our acquired wisdom to younger people so they can benefit from our experiences. As older adults, we have a strong need to reflect back on our previous stages, hopefully in a positive way.

Each stage has its own priorities, needs, challenges, and viewpoints. Therapists use this in their practices. We can use this information to understand others of a different generation better. We can also utilize this information to see our future and understand our past.

Now we can be more understanding of Grandpa's need to reminisce. But it will not help us understand the incessant need of Notre Dame graduates to do so.

Paris in the the Spring: Why We All Will Almost Hit the Guy on the Motorcycle

For over thirty years, I have written the following on the chalkboard (now the dry-erase board) of my introduction to psychology class: "Paris in the the spring." I have this on the board before the students come in. I then ask a student to read it aloud to the class. In thirty-plus years, no student has read it aloud correctly. Each time, it is read as "Paris in the spring." No one has ever read it aloud correctly as, "Paris in the the spring."

Why is this? We often see what we expect to see, not what is really there. We expect something on the board to make sense. So even though our eyes transmit the proper message to the brain, we interpret it differently, that is, in a way where it makes sense.

When we are at an intersection, we look left and look right. No cars are coming, and we pull out. And we almost run down some poor guy on a motorcycle. Why? The image of the cyclist was sent to the brain, but we did not notice him when we interpreted that information. We did not see the motorcyclist because we did not expect to.

If the Cubs win the World Series one day before the sun goes supernova, no one will see it. Why? Because he did not expect to.

I am Not a Bibliotherapist, But …

You can read a number of books where you can gain great insights into the human condition. They are motivating, insightful, and uplifting. You can obtain a great deal of useful and practical information from these books. Many are biographies or autobiographies.

- *Just Farr Fun* (Jamie Farr) provides great insights as to how to get along with others and yourself.

- *A Ragman's Son* (Kirk Douglas) is one of the most inspiring books you will ever read. It defines what courage really is.

- *Up Till Now* (William Shatner) says we should never give up and always move ahead.

- *Shatner Rules: Your Key to Understanding the Shatnerverse and the World at Large* (William Shatner) says you will experience a lot more if you (almost always) say yes to every opportunity. He. Really. Does. Not. Speak. Like. This.

- *Steve Jobs* (Walter Isaacson) says you can dream big and alter reality.

- *To the Stars: The Autobiography of George Takei* (George Takei) says we should make a plan and stick to it.

- *How I Got This Way* (Regis Philbin) says we can learn a lot from others if we let ourselves and that hard work always pays off.

- *We'll Be Here the Rest of Our Lives* (Paul Shaffer) says there is nothing wrong with being humble. The most successful usually are. When you love what you do, life is so much better.

- *Who Moved My Cheese?* (Spencer Johnson) says that we must embrace change in a modern, fast-changing world.

- *The One-Minute Manager* (Kenneth Blanchard) says that a good boss understands psychology and uses it. If you treat people well, they will work for you.

- *Looking Out for #1* (Robert Ringer) provides self-advocacy on steroids.

- *How to Win Friends and Influence People* (Dale Carnegie) teaches you how to do those two things and more. It's a timeless classic.

- *Life Itself* (Roger Ebert) is written by a man who never gives up. He demonstrates what real courage and honesty is. Roger Ebert admitted to some mistakes. That takes courage too.

- *The Art of Being Fully Human* (Leo Buscaglia) says that living life to its fullest, loving others, and giving to others is what life is all about.

It Is an Art and a Science

Psychology and the practice thereof is both an art and a science. To pretend otherwise is disingenuous. Admitting that psychology is part art does not diminish the field or its practitioner. Something as complex, sacred, and beautiful as human behavior and its study cannot be reduced to numbers only.

Practitioners of psychology make mistakes in the practice of their art. They are human, and all humans make mistakes. Claiming that psychology is just a science does not lessen the numbers of mistakes. When making a diagnosis, some psychologists, despite their training, will see what they expect to see rather than what is there. That is called being human. That does not mean we should not guard against this. But we should recognize that it occurs. Diagnosis and treatment can change from culture to culture or era to era. For example, homosexuality was once viewed as a sickness. Poor mothering was thought to cause autism. The science at the time led to these assumptions.

Recognizing that psychology is both an art and a science does not diminish the field or its adherents. I once worked at a clinic where we employed a prominent psychiatrist, one of the best in the field. On his first day, as a sort of hazing, I pretended to be his first patient because that person was a no-show. He was ready to hospitalize me, as I played the role of an extremely disturbed patient. Does that make him incompetent? No. It made him a practitioner attempting to ply his art that did his best under the circumstances.

Sometimes treatment is trial and error. Often, the efficacy of the treatment is determined more by the instincts and experience of the practitioner than the research. People are creative creatures, so practitioners must be creative as well. As society and culture change, so must the practitioner. Certainly, science advances—especially in light of the human genome project. But psychology will flourish if it advances as both an art and a science.

If we are honest about psychology being both art and science, we will be more careful because we should be. Taking the art out of the field lulls us into a false sense of security. Science can be wrong at times. What is accepted as science now may be disproved down the road as we advance. If we are open to psychology as being part art and part science, we leave room for the creativity that allows us to use our experience, compassion, and rapport with the patient and our judgment in human ways that can bridge the gap between what science does and does not yet know.

Flying Bananas

When I was a young suburban school psychologist, I sought extra contractual work summers in the big city. At the time, federal and state regulations required that a school psychologist reevaluate all students placed in special education every three years. A major U.S. city close to where I lived was looking for people like myself to complete these reevaluations over the summer.

The students I was to evaluate all had significant behavioral issues and were identified as having gang affiliations. I was asked to administer a certain battery of tests to each student, which included a test with a section of verbal absurdities. I would read to them a series of statements, some of them true and some of them absurdities, and the young man would simply answer yes or no as to if the statement were true. I suggested this particular test might not be appropriate for these specific students. I was told I would administer the specific test the school district had decided upon.

My first student came in. He was none too happy about the likes of me interrupting his summer. He made it clear that he did not want to be there and he wanted to get the testing over with as soon as possible. This was stated with rather salty language, and it was more like an ultimatum than a request. He was significantly larger than I was and truly had an intimidating demeanor.

In an effort to accommodate him, I jumped right into the testing and asked him the first question. "Do bananas fly?"

He looked at me with anger and shock before he asked me, "What the **** do you think?"

Then he grabbed me. I think I had it coming. I was right. That was not the best test to administer to these students. I hope they found someone else to do it.

That's life in the big city.

Not So Smart

Intelligence tests are good predictors of one's performance in school, but they have little, if anything, to do with how intelligent you are. If you have just learned English and take an IQ test, will you score low? Absolutely. Does that mean you are unintelligent? No. But the score will predict how well you will do in school (in an English-only program). Feeling creative? If you give an answer to a question on an IQ test that is not in the book, you will receive no credit. Regardless of how impressive your answer is, there will still be no credit. Creativity can lower your score.

The examiner asks you, "Why do we put stamps on letters?"

You reply, "Because if we don't, we cannot climb up them."

Such a series of answers will lower your score. You heard, "Why do we put steps on ladders?" Your IQ score will be lowered. Unintelligent? No. You have an auditory processing learning disability. The IQ score will probably be an accurate predictor of your school performance without the specialized support you need. An adequate indicator of your intelligence? Not so much.

Young children with very limited exposure and experience tend to score low on IQ tests. Are they unintelligent? Not necessarily. But again, these tests will probably do a good job of predicting how well that child will perform in school in the immediate future.

IQ tests and the scores they yield should be taken with a grain of salt. It's another example of psychology being an art and a science. When you admit it is, you tend to be more careful.

Is ADD a Desired Diagnosis?

Professionals who serve children must exercise due caution when labeling children as suffering from attention deficit disorder (ADD) or attention deficit/hyperactivity disorder (ADHD), the authors warn. Likewise, those who work in schools should refrain from implying that such a diagnosis absolves the child from all responsibility for his behavior in the school setting.

In case anyone has failed to notice, we live in a society that is rapidly being transformed. We all know about changes involving science, technology, and even human demographics. But many of us tend to overlook large changes taking place in the arena of social interaction, the often subtle manner in which individuals relate to one another. Sometimes, however, these interactions are not subtle at all and can lead to anxiety and conflict. When that happens, the disputants might resolve their own differences or seek professional help.

We also live in an age in which people seem preoccupied with finding an underlying cause for everything, especially in the areas of medical science and human behavior. Year after year, the medical profession forges ahead, offering the public new hope, potential cures, and new diagnoses. If you transplant this focus on underlying causes into psychology, we have a corresponding focus on new rationales for behavior.

Over the past decade or so, rationales have become very important to our modern theories of social interaction. Almost overnight, or so it seems, terms such as "guilty," "responsible," "liable," "self-control," and a plethora of others have become passé. Their use denotes the speaker as some type of ultraconservative reactionary. The use of some other terms, however, is on the rise. One hears more and more of "disorders," "afflictions," "dysfunctions," and "shared responsibility."

We suggest that, in the current atmosphere of acceptance and explanation, it is far easier to feel good about one's negative behaviors than it was fifty years ago. Doing a bad thing implies responsibility and guilt, as well as the need for some punitive action on the part of one's social peers. But having a dysfunction carries no such social stigma. Instead, it evokes sympathy, feelings of compassion, and a genuine desire to help the transgressor. From this, we suggest, comes the natural propensity of individuals to seek to escape from societal censure by claiming the role of victim as opposed to that of victimizer.

We can sense this change in the news every day. Bank robbers do not simply want an easy road to wealth. They are suffering from some type of compulsive behavior. Rapists are not sadistic opportunists with no sense of right and wrong. They have deep-seated doubts of their own sexuality, probably caused by some sort of abuse that we can ascribe to their parents or caretakers. We have seen the logical extension of all this. Patricide, matricide, and the hacking off of members of a spouse's body are acceptable behaviors as long as you can document that you have been the recipient of abuse. The list of negative behaviors that we as a society hold people responsible for is shrinking year by year, while the list of negative behaviors we ascribe to affliction grows ever longer.

We are all susceptible to this need to avoid blame. It is not confined to the criminal element. Indeed, it stems from a natural human desire to be well thought of. This is not lost on the children in our schools or their parents. Like the rest of us, they read the papers and watch the news on television. They are aware that placing blame on others is becoming politically incorrect in the contemporary social landscape. This social change is particularly appealing when Johnny comes home with yet another detention slip or when Sally throws her book across the classroom after being told to sit still.

39

If misbehaviors persist, Johnny and Sally will eventually be labeled as discipline problems and suspended for insubordination. All too often, such an action sparks a mad dash to the doctor's or psychologist's office in order to see if the discovery of some hidden malady can somewhat temper the "discipline problem" verdict. Lo and behold, the child emerges from this visit with a diagnosis of ADD or ADHD.

Whose Needs Are Being Met?

The rush to label schoolchildren as suffering from ADD or ADHD has reached nearly epidemic proportions. Currently, between 3 and 5 percent of U.S. students (1.35 million to 2.25 million children) have been diagnosed as having ADD. Is it time to investigate why this is happening? Perhaps more than one patient is making the trip to the doctor's office, the child with the discipline problem and the child's parents. After all, there is no definitive test for the disorder and no agreed-upon etiology. There are no blood tests to be run or X-rays to be taken. It would seem, at least on the surface, that people generally enjoy having their physician tell them that they have a clean bill of health and nothing is wrong with them. Why then do parents wish to come away with a diagnosis of ADD for their child?

The answer, of course, is that the diagnosis meets the needs of the parents more than it does those of the child. Almost at once, the parents feel relieved of some real or perceived pressures from educators, grandparents, and family friends. Having been unable to control the behavior of their children, they can now assign the control to Ritalin or some other drug. They are thus almost magically transformed into model parents. "I can't control you, son, but I have fulfilled my role as a parent by finding out what's wrong with you."

School personnel often feed into parents' desire for a medical diagnosis by holding off on any contemplated behaviorally disordered classification and directly or indirectly encouraging parents to seek medication. In short, all the adults seem happy that some dysfunction has been discovered, exactly the opposite of what our normal reaction would be if our doctors discovered any other malady.

In addition, a parent may be less than effective in some areas of parenting. Denial of this shortcoming on the part of parents is natural and to be expected. These parents may seek the ADD diagnosis because it lets them off the hook, so to speak. It focuses attention on the child and getting a prescription filled, not demanding any alteration of parents' behaviors or even any serious examination of them. The child now has a medical condition that has nothing to do with the child's upbringing. However, no parental introspection leads to no change in expectations or in conditions in the home. In this way, a diagnosis of ADD may not offset extremely negative conditions in a child's home that might best be served by the intervention of a social worker.

We are not questioning a physician's or psychologist's diagnosis of ADD. But we are suggesting that such a diagnosis be part of a total, wide-ranging investigation as to the conditions in which the child lives.

We have also noted that there is seldom, if ever, any reluctance on the part of the parents of ADD children to tell anyone within earshot that their child suffers from ADD. Sympathy is the usual reward for such utterances, and everyone likes sympathy. It is also a good statement to run by one's next-door neighbor the next time Bobby climbs over the fence and tramples the flower bed. We mustn't be too hard on the boy. After all, he's afflicted with ADD.

Popular magazines, television shows, and other media continually bombard parents with information on ADD. Many of these sources of information portray the disorder in such a way that virtually any youngster could be so classified. At one time or another, all children exhibit socially unacceptable behaviors. That is part of the maturation process. Anyone, even we professionals, can become hyperactive or distractible when forced to sit through a boring lecture or two. Going

41

on a shopping spree is certainly a type of impulsive behavior. Yet when we give in to such an impulse, we don't immediately classify ourselves as ADD.

To further complicate the issue, parents with very low incomes generally qualify for increased Medicaid or Supplemental Social Security Income benefits if their child is diagnosed as afflicted with ADD or ADHD. Does this offer an additional incentive to have one's child diagnosed thus? Are there individuals in this world who would encourage their children to act up in order to obtain more money?

Who Else Is Off the Hook?

Children are often more sophisticated than we give them credit for being. In this whole process, they are aware of what is going on. They are aware that the adults have found them difficult to handle. They are aware that conventional controls have not sufficed, and they are capable of working to sabotage the goals of those who would control them. Even if correctly labeled as ADD, the thinly veiled message that the child receives upon diagnosis is that he is somehow less responsible for his actions than the minute before the diagnosis was given.

Great care must be taken, lest this awareness become an excuse for every disruption under the sun. The fact that a child is taking Ritalin does not afford him a license to affect other students at school in negative ways. A diagnosis of ADD is not an excuse to hit other children or to sneer at the teacher. Distractibility and hyperactivity are more closely associated with involuntary behaviors. Waiting for another student after school in order to beat him up is most definitely a planned and voluntary action and should not be argued away by the aggressor's ADD classification.

Physicians and psychologists with ADD patients should exercise due caution when counseling the parents of afflicted children. A diagnosis of ADD can explain and even excuse certain negative behaviors, while others cannot. We must not lower our expectations for children because of the ADD diagnosis, or they will most certainly meet these lowered expectations. Lowered expectations can do great harm to a child. Given the fact that etiology and diagnosis are, at bottom, educated guesswork, this lowering of expectations for a child is not acceptable. Physicians should keep in close touch with the child's school in order to monitor the effect that the medication is having.

It is also unreasonable for school administrators to expect teachers to accommodate any type of aberrant behavior under the ADD umbrella. This distorts the ADD diagnosis, for ADD is not synonymous with behaviorally disordered. Therefore, children who are classified as ADD may also be considered for a special education evaluation if it is thought that their behaviors are beyond the realm of the ADD or ADHD spectrum.

Classroom teachers have the added responsibility of conveying to ADD students that, now that they are receiving help with their affliction, expectations for their classroom behavior will rise. After all, that is the purpose of medicating an ADD child, to bring that child into the circle of what is considered normative behavior. (And let us not forget that any sociologist can tell us that our definitions of "normative" often change dramatically from generation to generation.)

Adult counseling must also be a component of any ADD treatment. Children are experts at making excuses, and we do not want to give them the message that their classification as ADD or their being on medication affords them some added excuse whenever they get into trouble. We have to preserve the rights of the afflicted child's peers as well as the rights of the afflicted child. Physicians, psychologists, school officials, and teachers have an obligation to the child and his parents to explain that the classification of ADD or ADHD is not a license to get away with anything, but it is rather an explanation that may lead to legitimate help for the child in question.

An Edifice Built on Shifting Sand

We need to continually point out the facts that there is no concrete proof that the condition known as ADD even exists and that diagnosing the affliction remains more an art than a science. Moreover, the affliction seems to have no physiological basis. Although some correlation has been noted between fevers in early childhood and ADD, no causal connection has been proved, and the symptoms of ADD may indicate many other disorders, including a wide range of behavioral disorders.

When an etiology is not agreed on, a definitive test is not available, and only the efficacy of treatment seems to validate the initial diagnosis, then research typically abounds. But in the case of ADD, this has not held true. Clearly, more research is called for in order to determine whether a definitive test or series of tests is possible.

We also wish to point out that behavioral aberrations in children (and in adults, for that matter) seem to rise in societies whenever there is general disagreement as to whether or not people should be held responsible for socially unacceptable behaviors. In this context, it is interesting to note the experience of modern Russia when compared to that of the Soviet Union. Russian police report that elements of organized crime are infesting Moscow, something it did not experience under the Communist Party dictatorship. We are not here advocating police states or schools run as such, but it is curious to note how many people formerly had more control over themselves.

Now we are faced with an affliction that is based mainly on conjecture and is becoming increasingly popular in a society that is becoming increasingly conflicted with regard to differentiating between right and wrong. In an age in which discipline in the schools was strictly enforced, such afflictions or alleged afflictions were unknown. Children were, perhaps correctly and perhaps incorrectly, simply referred to as discipline problems and dealt with as such. It is probably safe to assume that, if we as a society continue to have problems deciding what one should or should not be held accountable for, we can expect to see a rise in the number of classified dysfunctions.

Simply stated, if excuses are courted and deliberately sought, then there will be no end of excuses available. This will be all the more lamentable if yet a further excuse for greater dysfunctional behavior lies embedded within each new excuse, leading to further diagnosis, more excuses, and so on.

To build a great medical/psychological edifice on such shifting sand seems ill advised. It would behoove educators and the medical and psychological professions alike to downplay the diagnosis of ADD, the potential benefits of medication, and the insulation that such diagnosis affords the patient from paying the price for poor behavior at school.

We feel the need to conclude with a statement that is highly controversial and, consequently, is seldom uttered. All children are not educable in the conventional sense, that is, within the walls of the school. Children are not interchangeable parts on a conveyor belt on a production line.

This does not necessarily mean that there is anything wrong with the children who do not conform. They may simply hate school. Adults tend to stick to tasks they dislike (sometimes for entire careers) because they have more self-control than children do and because they deem the rewards worth the distaste of the job. Children, being children, shun that which they find boring or distasteful, and their attention starts to wander. In short, not every human action (or lack of action) that is not identical to the actions of the majority can be attributed to some affliction. Such different behavior might just be the product of human choice. We must, therefore, be somewhat skeptical about ADD-classified children who, when removed from the classroom setting, magically lose their ADD symptoms.

The professions that serve these children, from the school to the doctor's office, must exercise due caution when labeling children as suffering from ADD or ADHD. Likewise, those of us who work in schools should refrain from implying that the diagnosis of ADD or ADHD absolves the child from all responsibility for his behavior in the school setting. In the reality of the workaday world, the individual is expected to cope with society to a greater degree than society is expected to cope with the individual. Children with negative social behaviors are classified and treated; adults are fired or arrested.

And Now the Breast of the Story

Breastfed children have higher IQs, are more resistant to many diseases, and can bond emotionally (in many cases) more effectively with their mothers. They often tend to socialize more effectively. These positives can range from small but measurable to very significant. Often overlooked are the emotional and physical benefits to mom. As positive as breastfeeding is for babies on so many levels, it just does not get the positive attention it deserves. It is a tremendously important factor in human development.

And now you know the rest of the story. Good day.

Smile!

Smiles involve more than showing happiness or pleasure. Research teaches us ways we can use them to our advantage. People are always smiling, but it doesn't simply mean they're happy. We use smiles for specific reasons because they can send out all sorts of signals that can be beneficial for us.

The following are some ways smiles can be used to our advantage by sending out messages about our physical attractiveness, trustworthiness, sociability, and more.

- **We often trust people that smile.** Who should we trust? Smiling suggests trustworthiness. Sincere smiles send a message that other people can trust and work with us. People who smile are rated as being more outgoing and even as being more generous.

- **Smiling can get us off the hook.** When we are caught doing something wrong, smiling can get us off the hook. People just won't be that angry with us.

- **We can recover from a social faux pas.** If we say or do something inappropriate, a smile conveys that we meant no harm. People can identify with that, and they tend to be more likely to forgive us.

- **We're supposed to.** When someone tells us a less than interesting story or enthusiastically shares with us an insight that is not all that insightful, we are supposed to smile. And people appreciate it.

- **It helps our emotions.** Our body takes cues from our facial expressions. If our facial expression is one of fear, we tend to be fearful. If our expression is one of pain, we often feel pain. If we smile, we feel better.

- **Smiling is insightful.** When we smile, we tend to have more insight into what we are thinking about. We actually concentrate better.

- **It attracts the opposite sex.** When women smile, men tend to approach them more.

- **It hides your feelings.** If you are good at faking a sincere smile, you can hide your true feelings.

- **You can smile to make money.** Waitresses have known for some time that touching a customer increases tips. Smiling does too. Both of them together are a good combination.

- **You can get people to smile back at you.** Most people will reciprocate a smile. If you smile at them, they will smile at you. This can dramatically increase the possibility of a pleasant interaction.

- **You can smile for health.** Research shows a statistical relationship between smiling and health. More smiling has a small but measurable impact on lifespan for some people.

Little Known Facts about Depression

1. Depression does not occur more often on holidays. It is more frequent in the summer.

2. When you are depressed, you do not reason well or make good decisions.

3. You are pretty self-centered when you are depressed. You do not think much about the needs of other people.

4. Many people who are extremely anxious are depressed and do not fully realize it.

5. If you are thin-skinned and easily offended and other people start bugging you, you may be depressed.

6. Often people who are frequently in pain are actually depressed.

7. Many people tend to self-medicate when depressed. An uptick in alcohol intake, for example, may indicate depression.

8. Depression can be very hard on the loved ones of the depressed person.

9. Exercise can positively impact mild depression. Ever hear of a runner's high?

10. If you are a fan of the Chicago Cubs, you will have a lifetime of depression and disappointment. Sneaking a goat into Wrigley Field may be the only effective cure.

11. Number 10 was not a serious fact about depression.

12. Yes, it is.

Lessons Learned

The study of human behavior, attempting to understand why we do what we do, is an area worthy of our attention and efforts. We will never fully comprehend it, and neither will anyone else. But striving to improve our knowledge of others and ourselves and making a lifelong commitment to do so is a good thing. It will help us be more understanding, patient, loving, and accepting. That's important and worth the effort.

CPSIA information can be obtained at www.ICGtesting.com
Printed in the USA
LVOW13s2345280414

383641LV00001B/68/P